IN THE LINE OF DUTY

An A to Z of Police Abbreviations and Acronyms

STRELLUS

CONTENTS

A

AABC
Action Against Business Crime 2008

AAIB
Air Accident Investigation Branch

ABA
Acceptable Behaviour Agreement

ABC
Agreed Behaviour Contract

ABCDE
Appearance Behaviour Communication Capacity Danger
& Environmental Circumstances

ABD
Acute Behavioural Disorder

ABD
Acute Behaviour Disturbance

ABE
Achieving Best Evidence

ABH
Actual Bodily Harm

ABI
Association of British Insurers

AC
Assistant Commissioner

ACAS
Advisory, Conciliation and Arbitration Service

ACC
Assistant Chief Constable

ACC
Anti-Corruption Command

ACD
Automatic Call Distribution

ACD
Automated Camera Detected

ACE
Asset Confiscation Enforcement

ACG
Automatic Call Distribution

ACP
Assistance Commissioner Professionalism

ACPC
Area Child Protection Committee

ACPIT
Assistant Commissioner Public Inquiry Team

ACPO
Association of Chief Police Officers (of England, Wales &
N Ireland)

ACPOS
Association of Chief Police Officers in Scotland

ACSC & O
Assistant Commissioner Specialist Crime & Operations

ACSO
Assistant Commissioner Specialist Operations

ACTP
Assistant Commissioner Territorial Policing

ADC
Additional Duties Commitment

ADCS
Association of Directors of Childrens Services

ADJ
Adjourned

ADMS

Alarm Data Management System

ADR
Annual Data Requirement

ADS
Accreditation Documentation Set

A & E
Accident & Emergency

AED
Automated External Defibrillators

AEP
Attenuated Energy Projectile

AEXPLO
Assistant Explosives Officer

AFI
Areas for Improvement

AFI
Authorised Firearms Inspector

AFO
Authorised Firearms Officer

AFPS
Armed Forces Pension Scheme

AFR

Automatic Fingerprint Recognition

AFT
Alternative Fitness Test

AFTC
Alternative Fitness Test Cycle

AFTT
Alternative Fitness Test Treadmill

AGS
Annual Governance Statement

AHORSETR
Assistant Horse Trainer

AI
Accident Investigator

AIO
Assistant Information Officer

AIU
Accident Investigation Unit

AJF
Adverse Judicial Findings

AL
Annual Leave

ALG

Association of London Governments

ALIB
Assistant Librarian

ALIBRARN
Assistant Librarian

ALO
Ambulance Liaison Officer

AMI
Apparent Mental Illness

AMIT
Area Major Incident Team

AML
Anti Money Laundering

AMPH
Approved Mental Health Professional

AMS
Applications Maintenance and Support

AMS
Applications Management Services

ANPR
Automatic Number Plate Recognition

AOABH

Assault Occasioning Actual Bodily Harm

AOR
Armed Operations Record

APA
Association of Police Authorities

APA
Advertising & Producers Association

APACS
Assessment of Policing and Community Safety

AP-APP
Armed Policing - Authorised Professional Practice

APLS
Automatic Personnel Location Systems

APP
Application

APP
Accredited Professional Practice

APRG
Armed Robbery Reference Group

APS
Acting Police Service

APV

Adolescent Parent Violence

APVA
Adolescent to Parent and/or Violence

AR
Annual Report

ARA
Assets Recovery Agency

ARC
Alarm Receiving Centres

ARCC
Aeronautical Rescue Coordination Centre

AR HELMET
Anti-Riot Helmet

ARL
Authority Revocation List

ARLS
Automatic Resource Location Systems

ARMS
Active Risk Management System

ARMS
Actuarial Risk Management System

Arqiva

Current Radio Service Supplier

ARV
Armed Response Vehicle

AS
All Stations

ASAP
As Soon As Possible

ASB
Anti Social Behaviour

ASBAP
Anti Social Behaviour Action Panel

ASBOs
Anti Social Behaviour Orders

ASCII
American Standard Code for Information Interchange

ASHE
Annual Survey of Hours and Earnings

ASO
Assistant Scientific Officer

ASP
Applications System Provider

ASTs

Arrest Support Teams

ASU
Air Support Unit

ASW
Approved Social Worker

ATOC
Association of Train Operating Companies

ATS
Automatic Traffic Signals

ATW
Access to Work

ATWM
Area Traffic Warden Manager

AVC
Additional Voluntary Contributions

AVL
Automatic Vehicle Location

AVLS
Automatic Vehicle Location Systems

AVS
Address Verification Service

AWARE

A Windows Application in a Resilient Environment

AWT
Affordable Workforce Targets

B

BARK
Brent Action for Responsible K9s

BAS
Business Access Services

BASS
Bail Accommodation Support Scheme

BAU
Business as Usual

BBM
Blackberry Messaging

BBP
Borough Based Policing

BCC
Block Check Character

BCC
Brigade Coordination Centre

BCDR

Business Continuity & Disaster Recovery Plan

BCH
Business Crime Hub

BCMUs
Borough Crime Management Units

BCP
Borough Crown Prosecutor

BCR
Borough Control Room

BCRP
Business Crime Reduction Partnership

BCS
British Crime Survey

BCTG
Borough Co-ordination & Tasking Group

BCTG
Borough Crime Tasking Group

BCU
Borough Command Unit

BDC
Business Development Co-ordinator

BDD

Borough Designated Despatch

BDO
Business Development Office

BDS
Boycott, Divestment and Sanctions

BECC
Borough Emergency Control Centre

BEEP
Building Energy Efficiency Programme

BEST
Behaviour Education & Support Teams

BF
Bring Forward

BFM
Borough Forensic Manager

BGSU
Borough Group Support Unit

BIA
Business Impact Assessment

BIAG
Black Independent Advisory Group

BIS

Bumblebee Imaging System

BIS
Business Innovation Skills

BIU
Borough Intelligence Unit

BIU
Business Intelligence Unit

BLO
Borough Liaison Officer

BME
Black or Minority Ethnicity

BNP
Bulgarian National Police

BOBB
Behave Or Be Banned

BOCC
Borough Olympic Command Centre

BOCU
Borough Operational Command Unit

(B) OCU
Borough & Operational Control Unit

BOS

Borough Operations Supervisor

BOTJ
Bringing Offenders to Justice

BPA
Black Police Association

BREEAM
Building Research Establishment Environment Assessment Method

BSIA
British Security Industry Association

BSMI
Borough Support Management Information

BSP
Borough Support Pool

BSU
Borough Support Unit

BT
British Telecom

BTAU
Business & Technical Assurance Unit

BTP
British Transport Police

BTR
Bail to Return

BVPI
Best Value Performance Indicator

BVR
Best Value Review

BVRI
Best Value Review Indicators

BVRLA
British Vehicle Rental and Leasing Association

BVR (T)
Best Value Review of Training

BWT
Borough Workforce Targets

BWT
Budgeted Workforce Targets

BWV
Body Worn Video

BZE
Benzoylecyonine

C

4Cs
Consult, Compare, Challenge & Complete

C3i
Command, Control, Communication and Information Project

CO11
Public Order OCU, Operations & Planning

CA
Confidentiality Agreement

CA
Custody Assistant

CA
Certificate Authority

CAA
Campaign Against Anti - Semitism

CAA
Comprehensive Area Assessment

CAADA
Co-ordinated Action Against Domestic Abuse

CAC
Central Ambulance Control

CAD
Communities Against Drugs

CAD
Computer Aided Despatch

CADMIS
Computer Aided Dispatch Management Information Systems

CADRE
Advanced Public Order Trained Officers

CAG
Communication Advisory Group

CAITS
Child Abuse Investigation Teams

CAIU
Civil Actions Investigation Unit

CALT
Centre of Applied Learning Technologies

CAMHS

Child & Adolescent Mental Heath Service

CAMHS
Child And Mental Health Service

C/ARB
Collision /Accident Report Book

CARE
Career Average Revalued Earnings

CARM
Computer Aided Resource Manager

CARMS
Computer Aided Resource Management System

CARPO
Communication And Press Relations Officer

CASO
Child Abuse and Sexual Offences Command

CAST
Centre for Applied Science and Technology

CAT
Community Action Teams

CAWNs
Child Abduction Warning Notices

CBDD

Centralised Borough Designated Despatch

CBOs
Criminal Behaviour Orders

CBRN
Chemical, Biological, Radiological & Nuclear

CBRNE
Chemical, Biological, Radiological, Nuclear and Explosive Incidents

CBSS
College Based Sandwich Student

CBT
Cognitive Behaviour Therapy

C & C
Command & Control

CC
Chief Constable

CCB
Central Casualty Bureau

CCC
Central Communications Command

CCCs
Community Consultation Coordinators

CCCC
Crown Court Case Clerk

CCCPTMG
Community Cohesion Contingency Planning and Tension Monitoring Group

CCG
Clinical Commissioning Group

CCI
Communications Control Interface

CCITT
International Telephony/Telegraphy Consultative Committee

CCMA
Call Centre Managers Association

CCN
Contract Change Number

CCO
Civilian Communication Officers

CCoA
CIPFA Common Chart of Accounts

CCP
Camera Control Protocol

CCRC
Criminal Cases Review Commission

CCRC
Criminal Cases Review Commission

CCRU
Cultural & Communities Resource Unit

CCS
Crown Commercial Services

CCS
Crime Control Strategy

CCTA
Central Computer & Telecommunications Agency

CCTV
Close Circuit Television

CCU
Cyber Crime Unit

C & D
Control & Direction

C & D
Command & Dispatch

C & D Act
Crime & Disorder Act

CDA
Controlled Drinking Zone Area

CDG
Corporate Development Group

CDI
Common Data Interface

CDLO
Controlled Drug Liaison Officers

CDO
Custody Detention Officers

CDOU
Central Driver Offences Unit

CDR
Commander

CDRP
Crime & Disorder Reduction Plan

CDRPs
Crime & Disorder Reduction Partnerships

CDS
Complaints & Discipline System

CDS
Corporate Demand Strategy

CED
Conductive Energy Devices

CENTREX
Central Police Training and Development Agency

CEO
Communications & Electronics Officer

CEO
Communications Enquiry Office

CEOP
Child Exploitation and Online Protection Centre

CESG
Communications Electronic Security Group

CERT-UK
Computer Emergency Response Team – United Kingdom

CEV
Cash Equivalent Value

CF
Carried Forward

CFO
Chief Financial Officer

CFoI
Campaign for Freedom of Information

CFO-MPS
Chief Financial Officer-Metropolitan Police Service

CFO-MOPAC
Chief Financial Officer-Mayors Office of Policing & Crime

CG
Consultancy Group

Ch Insp
Chief Inspector

Ch Supt
Chief Superintendent

CHI
Corporate Health Indicator

CHIS
Covert Human Intelligence Sources

CHS
Call Handling Service

CHS
Call Handling Service

CI
Chief Inspector

CIA
Community Impact Assessment

CIA
Confidentiality, Integrity and Availability

CIB
Complaints Investigations Bureau

CIBSE
Chartered Institute of Building Services Engines

CICA
Criminal Injuries Compensation Authority

CID
Criminal Investigation Department

CIDA
Concerned Inter-agency Drugs Action group

CIES
Comprehensive Income and Expenditure Statement

CIPFA
Chartered Institute of Public Finance and Accountancy

CIPP
Crime Investigation Priority Project

CIPT
Collisions Investigation Prosecution Team

CIO
Chief Information Officer

CIS
Consultancy and Information Service

CISD
Critical Incident Stress Debriefing

CISOs
Chief Information Security Officers

CIES
Comprehensive Income and Expenditure Statement

CIT
Crisis Intervention Teams

CIU
Casualty Information Unit

CIU
Collision Investigation Unit

CJ
Criminal Justice

CJA
Criminal Justice Act

CJO
Criminal Justice Office

CJOMS
Criminal Justice Offenders Management System

CJPU
Criminal Justice Protection Unit

CJS
Criminal Justice System

CJSG
Criminal Justice Strategy Group

CJSSS
Criminal Justice Simple Speedy Summary

CJU
Crime Justice Unit

CJX
Criminal Justice Extract

CJX
Criminal Justice Extranet

CKP
Certificate in Knowledge of Policing

CLA
Copyright Licensing Agency

CLAS
CSEG Listed Advisory Scheme

CLI
Calling Line Identity

CLIO
Central Logging of Intelligence Operations

CLO
Community Liaison Officer

CLO
Court Liaison Officer

CLP
Commissioner's Leadership Programme

CLPs
Casualty Landing Points

CLPD
Common Law Police Disclosure

CM
Configuration Management

CM
Conduct Matter

CMBVR
Crime Management Best Value Review

CMC
Central Mobilisation Centre

CMG
Community Monitoring Group

CMIB
Continuous Mortality Investigation Board

CMIS
Channel Management Information System

CMN
Community Monitoring Network

CMO
Chief Medical Officer

CMRU
Career Management & Retention Unit

CMS
Crime Management System

CMU
Crime Management Unit

CNC
Civil Nuclear Constabulary

CNN
Claim Control Note

CNs
Criminal Networks

CNPs
Custody Nurse Practitioners

CO
Central Operations

CO
Commissioner's Office

CO
Communications Officer

COBR
Cabinet Office Briefing Room

COFP
Conditional Offer Fixed Penalty

COG
Chief Officer Group

COLP
City of London Police

COMAH
Control of Major Accident Hazards

COMETS
Commissioner's Office METS (Civil Staff Sports & Social Association)

CONPHYS
Consulting Physician

CONTRLLR

CAD Controller

COP
Code of Practice

COP
Court of Protection

COP
College of Policing

COPA
Case Overview and Preparation Application

COPD
Chronic Obstructive Pulmonary Disease

CORIN
Correspondence on the Intranet

CorO
Coroner's Officer

Coroner
Coroner's Officer

Corres
Correspondence

COSHH
Control of Substances Hazardous to Health Regulations

COTS

Commercial off the Shelf

CP
Contingency Plan

CP
Certification Practice Statement

CPA
Christian Police Association

CPA
Critical Performance Area

CPAU
Corporate Performance Analysis Unit

CPCG
Crime Prevention Consultative Group

CPD
Continuous Professional Development

CPDA
Crime Prevention Design Adviser

CPEG
Community and Police Engagement Groups

CPIA
Criminal Procedure and Investigations Act 1996

CPIE

Crime Prevention Inclusion and Engagement

CPM
Coached Patrol Module

CPM
Commissioner of the Police of the Metropolis

CPM
Corporate Performance Meeting

CPO
Crime Prevention Officer

CPO
Commissioner's Private Office

CPS
Crown Prosecution Service

CPS
Certification Practice Statement

CPT
Child Protection Team

CPT
Central Purchasing Team

CPTDA
Central Police Training and Development Agency

CPU

Case Progression Unit

CPU
Child Protection Unit

CPV
Child Parent Violence

CQC
Care Quality Commission

CR
Community Resolution

C/R
Command / Response

CRA
Child Rescue Alert

CRAM
Children Risk Assessment Model

CRAMM
CCTA Risk Analysis and Management Method

CRB
Collision Report Book

CRB
Criminal Records Bureau

CRC

Community Rehabilitation Company

CRDMP
Crime Recording Decision Making Process

CRE
Commission for Racial Equality

CREV
Crime Related Exhibit Vouchers

CRIB
Crime Recording Investigation Bureau

CRIMINT
Criminal Intelligence

CRIP
Common Recognised Information Pictures

CRIS
Crime Report Information System

CRL
Certificate Revocation List

CRM
Customer Relationship Management

CRPV
Crime-Related Property Voucher

CRR

Community Race Relations

CRS
Calling Routing System

CRTP
Competence-Related Threshold Payment

CRW
Community Road Watch

CS
Crime Scene

CS
Corson and Stoughton Incapacitant Spray (CS Spray)

CSA
Central Station Alarm

CSA
Corporate Strategic Assessment

CSAS
Community Safety Accreditation Scheme

CSAZ
Community Safety Action Zones

CSC
Civil Service Compensation Scheme

CSC

Card Security Code

CSCI
Commission for Social Care Inspectors

CSE
Child, Sex Exploitation

CSE
Crime Scene Examiners

CSEW
Crime Survey for England and Wales

CSIS
Custody Suite Imaging System

CSM
Crime Scene Manager

CSMS
Customer Service Management System

CSP
Community Safety Partnership

CSP
Community Security Policy

CSR
Corporate Social Responsibility

CSS

Customer Satisfaction Survey

CSS
Costed Security Strategy

CSSP
Community Safety Strategic Partnership

CST
Community Safety Team

CST
Complaints Support Team

CST
Community Security Trust

CSU
Community Safety Unit

CT
Counter Terrorism

CTA
Call Routing Tower Agreement

CTC
Counter Terrorist Check

CTC
Counter Terrorist Command

CTI

Computer Telephony Integration

CTIB
Central Telephone Investigation Bureau

CTIO
Counter Terrorism Intelligence Officer

CTPNOC
Counter Terrorism Police National Operations Centre

CTSET
Communities Together Strategic Engagement Team

CTSFO
Counter Terrorism Specialist Firearms Officers

CU
Collation Unit

C-UAS
Counter-Unmanned Aerial System

CUSU
Communication Users Support Unit

CVF
Competency and Values Framework

CVS
Crime Victim Survey

CVU

Commercial Vehicle Unit

C & W
Cable & Wireless

CWSR
Calls Without Service Request

CYPS
Children & Young People's Services

CYPSG
Children & Young People's Strategy Group

CZ
Corporate Gazetteer

CTS
Career Transition Service

D

D4C
Driving for Change

DA
Domestic Abuse

DAAT
Drug Alcohol Action Team

DAC
Deputy Assistant Commissioner

DACSO
Deputy Assistant Commissioner Special Operations

DAMOVO
Current Telephony Supplier

DAMS
Digital Asset Management System

DAP
Diversity Awareness Programme

DARA
Directorate of Audit Risk and Assurance

DARIS
Demand and Resource Information System

DASM
Designated Adult Safeguarding Manager

DAT
Drug Action Team

DC
Detective Constable

D&C
Direction & Control

DCC
Detective Chief Contstable

DCC
Deputy Commissioners Command

DCC
Digital, Cyber and Communications

DCFD
Diversity and Citizen Focus Directorate

DCI
Detective Chief Inspector

DCNS
Deputy Commissioner for National Security

D/COMM
Deputy Commissioner

DCP
Deputy Commissioner's Portfolio

DCS
Detective Chief Superintendent

Det CH Supt
Detective Chief Superintendent

DDA
Disability Discrimination Act

DDI
Direct Dial Inward

DDM
Designated Disaster Mortuary

DDO
Designated Detention Officer

DECT
Digitally Enhanced Cordless Telephone

DEFRA
Department of Environment, Food and Rural Affairs

DEFS
Digital Electronic Forensic Services

Det Supt
Detective Superintendent

Dets
Details of the Investigation

DevNom
Development Nominal

DFLA
Democratic Football Lads Alliance

DHEP
Degree Holder Entry Programme

DHR
Domestic Homicide Review

DI
Detective Inspector

DIAG
Disability Independent Advisory Group

DIP
Drug Intervention Programme

DIPs
Discriminating Irritant Projectiles

DIR
Digital Interview Recorder

DIR
Duty Intelligence Researcher

DISC
Disconnect Command

DIU
Discrimination Investigation Unit

DIU
Divisional Intelligence Unit

DLS
Department of Legal Services

DM
Disconnect Mode

DMA
Divisional/Detainee Monies Account

DMC
Directorate of Media & Communications

DMM
Daily Management Meeting

DMPC
Deputy Mayor for Policing and Crime

DMS
Duties Management System

DNA
Deoxyribonucleic Acid

D/ND
Data / No Data Flag

DNS
Data Network Segment

DNT
Data Network Table

DOCO
Designing Out Crime Officers

DOI
Directorate of Information

DOIT
Development & Organisation Improvement Team

DOORs
Dynamic Object Orientated Requirements Systems

DOR
Directorate of Resources

DoT
Department of Transport

DP
Digital Policing

DP TOM
Digital Policing Target Operating Model

DPA
Data Protection Act 1998

DPA
Directorate of Public Affairs

DPCS
Department of Procurement & Commercial Services

DPG
Diplomatic Protection Group

DPLO
Divisional Press Liaison Officer

DPO
Data Protection Officer

DPP
Director of Public Prosecutions

DPPO
Designated Public Place Order

DPS
Directorate of Professional Standards

DPS SI
Directorate of Professional Standards – Specialist Investigations

DRA
Dynamic Risk Assessment

DRG
Drug Reference Group

DRM
Duty Resource Manager

DRM
Duty Resource Manager

DS
Detective Sergeant

DSA
Disability Services Association

DSA
Digital Signature Algorithm

DSA
Data Sharing Agreement

DSAP
Diversity Strategy Action Plan

DSC

Designated Security Co-ordinator

DSEI
Defence and Security Equipment International

DSI
Death or Serious Injury

DSMU
Diversity Strategy Monitoring Unit

DSO
Department Security Officer

D/Supt
Detective Superintendent

DSTL
Defence Science and Technology Laboratory

DSU
Development Support Unit

DSU
Discipline Support Unit

DSU
Dog Support Unit

DTC
Duty to Cooperate

DTD

Directorate of Training & Development

DTI
Department of Trade & Industry

DTO
Detention and Training Order

DTS
Diversity Training School

DTSU
Diversity Training Strategy Unit

DTTOs
Drug Treatment and Testing Orders

DTU
Divisional Training Unit

DV
Development Vetting

DV
Domestic Violence

DVA
Domestic Violence and Abuse

DVDS
Domestic Violence Disclosure Schemes

DVI

Disaster Victim Identification

DVLA
Driver and Vehicle Licensing Agency

DVOG
Domestic Violence Operation Group

DVPN
Domestic Violence Protection Notices

DVPO
Domestic Violence Protection Orders

DVWG
Domestic Violence Work Group

DWO
Dedicated Ward Officers

DWP
Department of Work and Pensions

E

EAA
Electoral Administration Act 2006

EAB
Evidence and Actions Book

EAH
Early Administration Hearings

EAP
Enterprise Architecture Platform

EBM
Evidential Breath Machine

EBP
Evidence Based Policing

EBTI
Evidential Breath Test Instrument

ECAT
European Communities Against Trafficking

ECB
Extended Control Byte

ECHR
European Court of Human Rights

ECM
Event Clear-up Method

ED
Expected Delivery

EDIT
Evidential Drug Identification Testing

EDL
English Defence League

EDM
Electronic Document Management

EDRM
Electronic Document and Records Management

EDU
Early Deletion Unit

E&E
Efficiency and Effectiveness

EEA
European Economic Area

EEK
Early Evidence Kits

EFH
Early First Hearing

EFP
European Firearms Permit

EFQM
European Foundation for Quality Management

e-GIF
e-Government Interoperability Framework

e-GMS
Electronic Government Metadata Standards

e-Government
Electronic Government

EHRC
Equality and Human Rights Commission

EIA
Equality Impact Assessment

EIDU
Events & Income Development Unit

EIR
Environmental Information Regulations

EISEC
Enhanced Information Service for Emergency Calls

ELS
Emergency Life Saving

ELS
Emergency Life Support

EM
Excellence Model

EMC
EEC Electromagnetic Compatibility

EMD
Emotional or Mentally Distressed

EMDR
Eye Movement De-sensitisation and Reprocessing

EMRO
Early Morning Restriction Orders

EMS
Environmental Management System

EMSCU
East Midlands Strategic Commercial Unit

EMT
Emergency Medical Technician

EOC
Emergency Operator Centre

EOD
Explosive Ordnance Disposal Unit

EPA
Emergency Planning Advisers

EPA
Enduring Powers of Attorney

EPDs
Electronic Personal Dosimeters

EPIC
Emergency Procedures and Information Centre

EPIC
Enforcement, Prevention Intelligence and Communication

EPMs
Emergency Planning Managers

EPO
Estate Police Officers

EPQ
Extended Project Qualification

EPU
Evaluation and Performance Unit

ER and R
Emergency Response and Recovery

ERAT
Electronic Risk Assessment Tool

ERM
Electronic Records Management

ERNIC
Earnings Related National Insurance Contributions

ERP

Enterprise Resource Management

ERP
Enterprise Resource Planning

ERPT
Emergency Response and Patrol Team

ERPT
Emergency Response Police Team

ERU
Employee Relations Unit

ERU
Evidence Recovery Unit

ES
Estates Strategy

ESB
Empress State Building

ESC
Escape Character

ESD
Electronic Service Delivery

ESD
Evidential Screening Data

ESMCP
Emergency Services Mobile Communications Programme

ESN
Emergency Service Network

ESP
Employer Supported Policing

ESPR
Environment Strategy and Progress Report

ET
Employment Tribunal

ETU
Employment Tribunal Unit

EU
European Union

EWMS
Emerald Warrant Management System

EWO
Education Welfare Officer

EWS
Embassy Warning System

EXPO
Explosives Officer

F

FACE
Fight Against Child Exploitation

FACPN
Forensic Adolescent Community Psychiatric Nurse

FACT
Federation Against Copyright Theft

FACTS
Focus Achievements Challenges Transitions Staff

FAL
Firearms Licensing

FALCON
Fraud and Linked Crime Online

FAQ
Frequently Asked Questions

FAT
Factory Acceptance Test

FATACC

Fatal Accident

FAW
Fairness at Work

FAWA
Fairness At Work Adviser

FAWAA
Fairness At Work Appeals Adviser

FBC
Fallback Control Facility

FBC
Final Business Case

FBI
Federal Bureau of Investigations

FBP
Finance Business Partners

FCA
Financial Conduct Authority

FCI
Forensic Collision Investigators

FCPs
Forward Command Points

FCR

Force Control Room

FCV
Forward Control Vehicles

FDC'S
Foundation and Development Centres

FDS
Force Development Services Limited

FET
Firearms Enquiry Team

FFA UK
Financial Fraud Action UK

FI
Forensic Investigator

FIHWs
First Instance Harassment Warnings

FINDS
Forensic Information Database Services

FIPS
Federal Information Processing Standards

FISP
MPS Information Security Policy

FIT

Forward Intelligence Team

FIU
Financial Investigation Unit

FLA
Football Lads Alliance

FLA
Family Liaison Adviser

FLC
Family Liaison Co-ordinator

FLM
Family Liaison Manager

FLO
Family Liaison Officer

FM
Facilities Management

FMCP
Financial Management Code of Practice

FME
Forensic Medical Examination

FME
Forensic Medical Examiner

FMECA

Failure Mode, Effects and Criticality Analysis

FNBD
Fix Need By Date

FPN
Fixed Penalty Notice

FOD
Filed on Division

FOG
Fraudulently Obtained Genuine

FOI
Freedom of Information

FOIA
Freedom of Information Act 2000

FOS
Financial Ombudsman Service

FPU
Firearms Policy Unit

FQDN
Federal Information Processing Statement

FQDN
Fully Qualified Domain Name

FRACAS

Failure Reporting And Corrective Action System

FRM
Finance and Resources Manager

FRMR
Frame Reject Command

FRP
Forensic Readiness Policy

FRRC
Friends and Relatives Reception Centre

FSB
Federation of Small Businesses

FSHC
Four Seasons Health Care

FSP
Forensic Service Providers

FSR
Forensic Science Regulator

FTA
Fault Tree Analysis

FTE
First Time Entrants

FTE

Full Time Equivalent

FTRS
Full-Time Reservists Service

FVA
Full Viability Assessment

G

GCJU
Glidewell Criminal Justice Unit

GDPR
General Data Protection Regulation

GDSC
Government Data Standard Catalogue

GDST
Girls Day School Trust

GFLB
Gravity Friction Lock Baton

GH
Gifts and Hospitality

GIS
Geographic Information System

GMP
Greater Manchester Police

GMU

General Message Unit

GOL
Government Office for London

GP
General Practitioner

GPG
Good Practice Guide

GPS
Global Positioning System

GRC
Gender Recognition Certificate

GRITS
Gang Related Incident Tracking System

GS
General Support

GSC
Government Security Classification

GSZ
Government Security Zone

GTLOs
Gypsy and Traveller Liaison Officers

GTN

Government Telecommunications Network

GUI
Graphical User Interface

H

HAC
Humanitarian Assistance Centre

HARPs
Housing Association Registered Providers

HASWA
Health And Safety at Work Act

HAZMAT
Hazardous Material

HBA
Honour Based Abuse

HBPOS
Health Based Places of Safety

HBV
Honour Based Violence

HCI
Human Computer Interface

HCLO

Hate Crime Liaison Officer

HCP
Health Care Professional

HCVA
Hate Crime Victims Advocates

HDLC
High Layer Data Link Control Procedure

HEAD
Health, Education Accommodation and Drugs Team

HEMS
Helicopter Emergency Medical Service

HH
Half Hour

HM
Her Majesty

HMCE
Her Majesty's Customs and Excise

HMCG
Her Majesty's Coast Guard

HMCPSI
Her Majesty's Crown Prosecution Service Inspectorate

HMCTS

Her Majesty's Courts and Tribunal Services

HMEPOs
Hazardous Material and Environmental Protection Officers

HMG
Her Majesty's Government

HMIC
Her Majesty's Inspectorate of Constabulary

HMIC (T)
Her Majesty's Inspectorate of Constabulary - Training

HMICFRS
Her Majesty's Inspectorate of Constabulary and Fire & Rescue Services

HMIS
Her Majesty's Immigration Service

HMPPA
Her Majesty's Prisons and Probation Service

HMSO
Her Majesty's Stationery Office

HO
Home Office

HOC
House of Commons

HOCR
Home Office Counting Rules

HOG
Home Office Guidance

HOIE
Home Office Immigration Enforcement

HOL
House of Lords

HOLMES
Home Office Large Major Enquiry System

HomRAG
Homicide Research Action Group

HORT
Home Office Road Traffic

HOSOL
Home Office Serious Offence List

HPDS
High Potential Development Scheme

HQ
Headquarters

HR
Human Resources

HRA
Human Rights Act

HRM
Human Resources Manager

HSCIC
Health and Social Care Information Centre

HSE
Health and Safety Executive

HSM
Hardware Security Module

HUA
Hold Up Alarm

I

IAAC
Information Assurance Advisory Council

IAG
Independent Advisory Group

IAM
Islamophobic Awareness Month

IAO
Information Asset Owner

IAR
Information Asset Register

IASB
Information Assurance and Security Board

IASC
Independent Anti-Slavery Commissioners

IAT
Inter Agency Talk Groups

IAU
Information Assurance Unit

IB
Intelligence Bureau

IBO
Integrated Borough Operations

IC
Identification Code

IC
Information Commissioner

ICAS
Intelligence Cell Analysis System

ICB
Impact Co-ordination Board

ICC
Incident Call Handling Centre

ICCS
Integrated Communications and Control Systems

ICF
Integrated Client Function

ICG
Independent Challenge Group

ICO
Information Commissioner's Office

ICP
Independent Challenge Panel

ICP
Integrated Communication Platform

ICPO/Interpol
International Criminal Police Organisation

I/C Public
In-Coming Public Call

ICRP
Islington Crime Reduction Partnership

ICRW
International Centre for Research on Women

ICT
Information / Communications Technology

ICV
Independent Custody Visitors

IDG
Intelligence Development Group

IDO
Identification Officer

IDR
Incident Data & Resources

IDS
Internal Despatch System

IDT
Interpreter Deployment Team

IDVA
Independent Domestic Violence Advocates

IETF
Internet Engineering Task Force

IEU
Incident Enquiry Unit

IEX
Interim Exemption Scheme

IFAC
International Federation of Accountants

IFRS
International Financial Reporting Services

IGF
Information Governance Framework

IGIP
Integrated Gang Intervention Project

IHRA
International Holocaust Remembrance

IHRS
Ill Health Retirement Secretariat

IIC
Internal Investigations Command

IICSA
Independent Inquiry into Child Sexual Abuse

IIO
Initial Investigation Officer

IIP
Integrated Intelligence Platform

IIP
Investors in People

IIR
Immediate Informal Resolution

IKWRO
Iranian and Kurdish Women's Rights Organisation

ILMCS
Inner London Magistrates Courts Service

ILPS
Inner London Probation Service

IM
Information Manager

IM
Information Management

IMB
Information Management Board

IMB
Information Management Branch

IMBA
Information Management Business Area

INFOSEC
Information Security

Insp
Inspector

IO
Investigating Officer

IO
Investigation Officer

IOCCO
Interception of Communication Commissioner's Office

IOPC
Independent Office for Police Conduct

IOTA
Investigating Officer Throughput Analysis

IOWA
Investigating Officer Workload Analysis

IP
Incident Print

IPCC
Independent Police Complaints Commission (Now replaced by the Independent Office for Police Conduct (IOPC))

IPF
Information Policy Framework

IPG
Information Programme Group

IPI
Improvement of Police Information

IPLDP
Initial Police Learning and Development Programme

IPM
Information Policy Model

IPMS
Institute of Professionals, Managers & Specialists

IPO
Intervention Programme Officer

IPS
Independent Patrol Status

IPSAS
International Public Sector Reporting Standards

IPT
Integrated Prosecution Teams

IR
Informal Resolution

IR
Information Room

I & R
Inspection & Review

IRAS
Information Risk Appetite Statement

IRB
Incident Report Book

IRIS
Integrated Rainbow Information System

IRS
Intermediate Routing Site

IRSG
Inquiry and Review Group

IRSC
Inquiry and Review Support Command

IRT
Identification, Referral and Tracking system

IRT
Intervention Response Team

IRV
Instant Response Vehicle

IS
Information Systems

IS
Information Security

ISA
Information Sharing Agreement

ISAB
Information Security and Assurance Board

ISB
Impact Statements for Business

ISCF
Information Systems Compliance Framework

ISDP
Investigation Supervisors Development Programme

ISN
Islington Survivors Network

ISO
International Standards Organisation

ISO
Information Security Officer

ISP
Information Strategy Programme

ISPOs
Interim Stalking Protection Act 2019

ISSP
Intensive Supervision & Surveillance Programme

ISS4PS
Information Systems Strategy for the Police Service

ISTV
Information Sharing to Tackle Violence

ISVA
Independent Sexual Violence Advisers

IT
Industrial Tribunal

IT
Information Technology

I&T
Integrated & Test

ITHC
Information Technology Health Check

ITL
Integration Test Laboratory

ITSM
IT System Management

ITT
Invitation to Tender

IVA
Initial Viability Assessment

IVMA
In Vehicle Mobile Application

IVMD
In Vehicle Mobile Devices

IVR
Interactive Voice Response

IYSS
Integrated Youth Support Service

IHR
Ill Health Retirement

J

JD
Judicial Disposal

JDM
Joint Decision Makers

JEDI
Joint Enforcement Development Initiatives

JESCC
Joint Emergency Services Control Centre

JESIP
Joint Emergency Services Interoperability Programme

JHRW
Jewish Human Rights Watch

JPM
Joint Performance Management

JRFT
Job Related Fitness Test

JRU
Joint Response Unit

JSJD
Justice Seen Justice Done

K

KIISMET
Knowledge Information Intelligence Solutions for the MPS

KIN
Key Individual Network

KLOE
Key Lines of Enquiries

KPI
Key Performance Indicator

KPRM
Key Performance Review Meetings

KREs
Knowledge Retention Examinations

KSI
Killed or Seriously Injured

KYC
Know Your Customer

L

LAA
Local Authority Agreement

LAA
London Air Ambulance

LAC
Looked After Children

LALO
Local Authority Liaison Officer

LAN
Local Area Network

LASPO
Legal Aid, Sentencing and Punishment of Offenders Act 2012

LBPR
Lawful Business Practice Regulations

LCD
Lord Chancellors Department

LCJB
Local Criminal Justice Board

LCS
Language Cultural Service

LCV
Light Commercial Vehicles

LDAP
Lightweight Directory Access Protocol

LDC
Learning Delivery Centre

LDSS
Locally Delivered Support Services

LEA
Local Education Authority

LFMS
Linguistic and Forensic Medical Services

LGBTAG
Lesbian, Gay, Bisexual & Transgender Advisory Group

LGV
Large Goods Vehicle

LIB
Librarian

LIN
Local Information Notepads

LIO

Local Intelligence Officer

LIP
Leading Investigation Programme

LOEG
Licensing Operational Enforcement Group

LPA
Lasting Powers of Attorney

LPM
Local Policing Model

LQC
Legally Qualified Chair

LRADS
Long Range Acoustic Devices

LROs
Lead Responsible Officers

LSABs
Local Safeguarding Adults Boards

LSB
Least Significant Bit

LSC
Local Security Champion

LSGC
Long Service and Good Conduct

LSN

Least Significant Nibble

LSO
Licenced Search Officer

LSOA
Lower Super Output Area

LSP
Local Strategic Partnership

LTS
Long Term Sickness

M

MACC
Military Aid to Civil Community

MACP
Military Aid to Civil Power

MAGD
Military Aid to Other Government Departments

MAHA
Multi Agency Holding Area

MAMA
Multi Agency Marshalling Area

MAMA
Measuring Anti-Muslim Attacks

MAMA
Monitoring Anti-Muslim Attacks

MAP
Mobile Aware Project

MAP
Microsoft Accelerate Programme

MAPPA
Multi-Agency Public Protection Agreements

MAPPS
Multi-Agency Public Protection Panels

MARAC
Multi-Agency Risk Assessment Conferencing

MARIA
Mothers Against Radical Islam and Sharia

MASH
Multi-Agency Support Hub

MASH
Multi-Agency Safeguarding Hub

MASTS
Mobile Armed Support to Surveillance Officers

M&CA
Misconduct & Civil Actions Command

MCA
Maritime and Coastguard Agency

MCF
Major Change Fund

MCMI
Misconduct and Complaints Management Information

MCPRF
Metropolitan and City Police Relief Fund

MCRAC
MET Wide Crimint Remote Access

MCSSS
Metropolitan Civil Staffs Superannuation Scheme

MCVs
Mobile Control Vehicles

MDP
Ministry of Defence Police

MDT
Mobile Data Terminal

MEAT
Most Economical Advantageous Tender

MEND
Muslim Engagement and Development

MERIT
Mobile Emergency Response Incident Team

Met
Metropolitan Police Service

METADATA
Data About Data

Met AIR
MPS Accident Information Reporting

MetCU
MPS Circulation Unit

METTUS
MPS Trade Union Side

MG
Manual of Guidance file preparation forms

MHA
Mental Health Act

MI
Major Incident

MI
Management Information

MICC
Management Information and Communication Centre

MIR
Major Incident Room

MIRSAP
Major Incident Room Standardised Administrative Procedures

MIS
Management Information System

MISPER
Missing Persons

MIT
Major Investigation Team

MIT

Murder Investigation Team

MMR
Monthly Management Report

MMR
Monthly Monitoring Report

MO
Medical Officer

MOD
Ministry of Defence

MOG
Manual of Guidance

MOPAC
Mayor's Office for Policing and Crime

MoPI
Management of Police Information

MOSOVO
Management of Sexual and Violent Offenders Course

MOU
Memorandum of Understanding

MOWP
Making Of Without Payment

MP
Member of Parliament

MP-SOR

MPS Specialist Operations Room

MPS
Manual of Protective Security

MPS
Mailing Preferences Service (The)

MPU
Marine Policing Unit

MSA
Mass Spec Analytical

MSB
Most Significant Byte

MSF
Muslim Safety Forum

MSL
Maternity Support Leave

MSN
Most Significant Nibble

MSO
Message Switch Office

MSP
Managed Services Provider

MSS
Message Switching Service

MSSR
Multi Stage Shuttle Run

MSU
Marine Support Unit

MSV
Most Serious Violence

MTBF
Mean Time Between Failure

MTFP
Medium Term Financial Plan

MTI
MPS Technology Infrastructure

MTIP
More Through with Intimate Parts

MTP
Master Test Plan

MTPAS
Mobile Telephony Priority Access System

MV
Management Vetting

MHAA
Mental Health Act Assessment

N

NAAN
National Appropriate Adult Network

NACRO
National Association for Care and Resettlement of Offenders

NAD
Not Another Drop

NAFIS
National Automated Fingerprint Identification System

NAMI
National Alliance of the Mentally Ill

NAMP
National Association of Muslim Police

NAO
National Audit Office

NASCH
Name, Age, Sex, Colour, Height

NCALT
National Centre of Applied Learning Technology

NCDV
National Centre for Domestic Violence

NCIS
National Criminal Intelligence Service

NCM
National Costing Model

NCMS
National Contact Management System

NCRs
Non-Catalogue Requests

NCRS
National Crime Record Standards

NCSC
National Cyber Security Centre

NCSP
National Cyber Security Programme

NCTP
National Counter Terrorism Policing HQ

NCTT
National Community Tension Team

NDAC
National Driver Awareness Course

NDIS
National Driver Improvement Scheme

NDM
National Decision Model

NDORS
National Drivers Offenders Retraining Scheme

NDUC
Norwegian Defence University College

NF
National Front

NFA
No Further Action/ No Fixed Abode

NFIB
National Fraud Intelligence Bureau

NFIS
National Fingerprint Image System

NFO
National Fingerprint Office

NFRN
National Federation of Retail Newsagents

NFS
National Fire Standard

NGD
Next Generation Desktop

NGLP
National Graduate Leadership Programme

NGOS
Non-Governmental Organisations

NHH
Non Half Hour

NHS
National Health Service

NHSLA
NHS Litigation Authority

NI
National Indicator

NICC
National, International Capital City Funding

NICE
National Institute for Clinical Excellence

NIE
National Investigation Exam

NIM
National Intelligence Model

NIP
Notice of Impending Prosecution

NIS
National Indicator Set

NJG
Narrowing the Justice Gap

NLA
Newspaper Licensing Agency

NLSF
National Legal Services Framework

NMUS
National Managed Uniform Services

NNDR
National Non-Domestic Rates

NONDC
Norwegian National Defence College

NOMS
National Offenders Management System

NOS
Notifiable Occupation Scheme

NPA
National Police Air Service

NPAS
National Police Air Service

NPCC
National Police Chief's Council

NPCE
National Centre for Policing Excellence

NPIA
National Policing Improvement Agency

NPIRMT
National Police Information Risk Management Team

NPOCC
National Police Coordination Centre

NPP
National Police Plan

NPPF
National Police Promotion Framework

NPPF
National Planning Policy Framework

NPPS
New Police Pension Scheme

NPPV
Non-Police Personnel Vetting

NPS
National Probation Service (The)

NPSA
National Patient Safety Agency

NPSAT
National Protective Services Analysis Tool

NPT
National Police Training

NRAC
National Retention Assessment Criteria

NRCPD
National Registers of Communications Professionals working with Deaf and Deaf Blind People

NRM
National Referral Mechanism

NRS
National Recruitment Standards

NSAC
National Speed Awareness Course

NSAC20+
National Speed Awareness Course for 20mph

NSIRO
National Senior Information Responsible Officer

NSLEC
National Specialist Law Enforcement Centre

NSPCC
National Society for Prevention of Cruelty to Children

NSPIS
National Strategy for Police Information Systems

NSPIS
National Strategy for Police Information Services

NTA
Network Tower Agreement

NTE

Nightime Economy

NTL
Former Radio Service Supplier (Now Arqiva)

NSY
New Scotland Yard

NTFIU
National Terrorist Financial Investigation Unit

NUMS
National Uniformed Managed Service

NYPD
New York Police Department

O

OBIEE
Oracle Business Intelligence Enterprise Edition

OBTJ
Offences Brought to Justice

OCG
Operational Command Group

OCG
Organised Crime Group

OCGM
Organised Crime Group Mapping

OCJR
Office of Criminal Justice Reform

OCSP
Online Certificate Statue Protocol

OCU
Operational Command Unit

ODA

Online Dating Association

OEP
Operational Event Planner

OFSTED
Office for Standards in Education, Children's Services and Skills

OGC
Office of Government Commerce

OH
Occupational Health

OHA
Occupational Health Adviser

OHCH
Online Hate Crime Hub

OHM
Occupational Health Manager

OIC
Officer In Charge

OIC
Officer In the Case

OID
Object Identifier

OJEU
Official Journal of the European Union

OM
Operational Monitor

Op Eval
Operation Evaluation

OPG
Office of the Public Guardian

OPM
Operational Patrol Module

OPM
Operational Policing Measure

OPS
Operations

OPSU
Operational Policing Support Unit

OSA
Official Secrets Act

OSAC
Overseas Security Advisory Council

OSD
Olympic Security Directorate

OSS
Operational Specialist Support - (Air Support Unit, Marine Support Unit & Dog Support Unit)

OST
Officer Safety Training

OST
Operational Safety Training

OTIS
Operational Technology Information Service

OTIS
Operational Technology Support Unit

OTSU
Operational Technology Support Unit

OU
Open University

OVCU
Organised Vehicle Crime Unit

OVRO
Overseas Visitors Records Office

P

PABEN
Police Advisory Board of England and Wales

PABX
Private Automatic Branch Exchange

PAC
Pre-Assessment Checklist

PACs
Police Action Checklists

PACE
Police And Criminal Evidence Act 1984

PACT
Parents and Abducted Children Together

PANIU
Plant, Agricultural, National, Intelligence Unit

PAO
Public Access Office

PAO

Public Affairs Office

PAP
Procurement Assurance Process

PaRT
DPS Prevention and Reduction Team

PAS
Public Access Space

PAS
Public Attitude Survey

PASF
Police Approved Secure Facility scheme

PAT
Positive Action Team

PAT
Procurement Assurance Team

PATP
Proactive Assessment and Tasking Performa

PBO
Permanent Beat Officers

PBX
Private Branch Exchange

PC

Personal Computer

PC
Police Constable

PCA
Parental Control Agreement

PCA
Police Complaints Authority

PCC
Police and Crime Committee

PCCG
Police & Community Consultative Group

PCDAs
Police Constable Degree Apprenticeships

PCFT
Police Constable Foundation Training

PCH
Policy Clearing House

PCKI
Public Complaints Key Indicators

PCM
Prevent Case Management

PCS

Public and Commercial Services Union

PCSO
Police Community Safety Officer

PCSO
Police Community Support Officers

PCSPS
Principal Civil Service Pension Scheme

PCT
Primary Care Trust

PD
Personality Disorder

PDA
Personal Digital Assistant

PDD
Professional Development Day

PDF
Portable Document Format (Adobe Acrobat)

PDR
Personal Development Review

PDR
Performance Development Review

PDSU

Police Driver Standard Unit

PDT
Programme Delivery Team

PDU
Professional Development Unit

PECS
Prisoner Escort Contracted Service

PEEPs
Personal Emergency Evacuation Procedures

PELF
Palesta Event Liaison Facility

PEQF
Policing Education Qualifications Framework

PER
Prisoner Escort Record

PFA
Partnership Framework Agreement

PFI
Private Finance Initiative

PGA
Police Geographical Area

PGT

Pan Government Thesaurus

PHE
Public Health England

PHMF
Public Health Mortality File

PI
Performance Indicator

PI
Personal Injury (Road Accident)

PIA
Privacy Impact Assessment

PIAB
Police Information Assurance Board

PICD
Post Incident Coordination Desk

PIANO
Personal Injury Accident Notification Online

PIB
Performance Information Bureau

PID
Project Initiation Document

PIM

Post Incident Manager

PIMS
Personnel Information Management Systems

PINs
Police Information Notices

PIO
Police Incident Officer

PIP
Professional Investigation Programme

PIT
Public Interest Test

PITO
Police Information Technology Organisation

PKI
Public / Private Key Infrastructure

PKCS
Public Key Cryptosystem Standards

PLAIT
Parliamentary Liaison And Investigation Team

PLO
Prosecution Liaison Officer

PLO

Prison Liaison Officer

PLP
Press Liaison Point

PM
Personnel Manager

PM
Project Manager

PMA
Policy Management Authority

PMBS
Police Main Base Station

PMP
Partnership Management Process

PMP
Protective Monitoring Plan

PMS
Protective Marking System

PNA
Performance Needs Analysis

PNAC
Police National Assessment Centre

PNB

Police Negotiation Board

PNBs
Personal Notebooks

PNBs
Pocket Notebooks

PNC
Police National Computer

PNCB
Police National Computer Bureau

PNCID
Police National Computer Identification

PND
Penalty Notice for Disorder

PNICC
Police National Information Coordination Centre

PO
Public Order

POCA
Proceeds of Crime Act

POCET
Public Order and Civil Enquiry Team

POLACC

Police Accident

POLCOLL
Police Collision

POLE
Person Object Location Event

POLSA
Police Search Adviser

POSC
Public Order Strategic Committee

POTC
Public Order Training Centre

POU
Police Organisation Unit

PP
Policing Priority

PPAF
Police Property Act Fund

PPAF
Policing Performance Assessment Framework

PPCMT
Pay and Pensions Contract Management Team

PPD

Public Protection Desk

PPE
Personal Protective Equipment

PPERA
Parties Political Elections and Referendum Act 2000

PPK
Personal Protective Kit

PPM
Potential and Potential Matrix

PPO
Prolific Priority Offender

PPRC
Planning, Performance, Review Committee

PPS
Police Pension Scheme

PPSG
Public Protection Steering Group

PPTs
Prisoners Processing Teams

PPU
Public Protection Unit

PPV

Prisoners Property Voucher

PQQ
Pre-qualification Questionnaire

PR
Personal Radio

PR
Police Regulations

PRA
Public Records Act

PRA
Police Reform Act

PRC
Performance Review Committee

Predpol
Predictive Policing

PRO
Persistent Road Offenders

PROOF
Protected Online Filing

PromNom
Prominent Nominal

PRRA

Pre-Release Risk Assessment

PRRB
Police Remuneration Review Body

PRS
Performance and Review Service

PRS
Policy Review Standards

PRU
Performance Review Unit

PS
Personal Secretary

PS
Police Sergeant

PSAs
Public Service Agreements

PSCC
Professional Standards and Complaints Committee

PSCs
Professional Standards Champions

PSD
Property Service Department

PSD

Property Service Directorate

PSDB
Police Scientific and Development Branch

PSED
Public Sector Equality Duty

PSG
Personnel Security Group

PSMA
Public Service Mapping Agreement

PSPL
Post Staff Posting List

PSOs
Problem Solving Officers

PSP
Problem Solving Process

PSPO
Public Space Protection Order

PSR
Pre-Sentence Report

PSU
Police Support Unit

PSUs

Professional Standards Unit

PSSC
Professional Standards Strategic Committee

PSSO
Police Skills and Standards Organisation

PSTN
Public Switched Telephone Network

PSV
Public Service Vehicle

PTDB
Police Training Development Board

PTF3
Partnership Task Force 3

PTIU
Pathfinder Telephone Investigation Unit

PTO
Public Telecommunication Operator

PTR
Programme Trouble Reports

PTRB
Programme Trouble Report Board

PTSD

Post-Traumatic Stress Disorder

PTT
Press to Talk

PTW
Powered Two Wheelers

PTZ
Pan, Tilt and Zoom

PUoF
Police Use of Firearms

PURE
Police Use of Resources Evaluation

PYTD
Police Year to Date

PYO
Persistent Young Offenders

Q

QA
Quality Assurance

QCS
Quality Control Supervisor

QPM
Queen's Police Medal

QSR
Quality of Service Report

QU
Quality Report

R

RA
Registration Authority

RAC
Resource Allocation Committee

RAF
Resource Allocation Formulae

RAF
Royal Air Force

RAG
Red Amber Green system

RAIL
Resources Allocation & Incident Logging

RAO
Registration Authority Operator

RARTS
Regional Assets Recovery Teams

RAYNET
Radio Amateurs Emergency Network

RBF
Registry Bring Forward

RCA
Route Cause Analyse

RCCO
Revenue Contribution to Capital

RCIO
Regional Crime Intelligence Officer

RCS
Regional Crime Squad

RCT
Randomised Control Trail

RDD
Radiological Dispersion Device

RDPD
Royalty & Diplomatic Protection Department

RES
Race Equality Scheme

RF
Routing Failure

RFD
Registered Firearms Dealer

RFFI

Requests For Further Information

RIC
Remand in Custody

RIC
Rail Incident Commander

RIDDOR
Reporting of Injuries, Diseases & Dangerous Occurrences
Regulations

RIDE
Rider Intervention Developing Experience (Powered
two wheelers)

RIO
Rail Incident Officer

RIP
Retention Improvement Project

RIPA
Regulation of Investigatory Powers Act 2000

RJ
Restorative Justice

RMADS
Risk Management Accreditation Document Set

RMB
Records Management Branch

RMC
Resource Managment Centre

RMC
Racially Motivated Crime

RMG
Royal Mail Group

RMM
Records Management Manual

RMS
Records Management System

RMS
Resources Management System

RNLI
Royal National Lifeboat Institution

RO
Registration Officer

ROCUs
Regional Organised Crime Units

ROWD
Reporter of Wrong Doing

RPA
Representation of the People Act 1983

RPT
Roads Policing Teams

RR (A) A
Race Relations (Amendment) Act 2000

RRD
Review, Retention and Disposal

RRG
Rape Reference Group

RSPCA
Royal Society for the Prevention of Cruelty to Animals

RSG
Revenue Support Grant

RSL
Registered Social Landlords

RSO
Registered Sex Offender

Rt Hon
Right Honourable

RTA
Road Traffic Act/Road Traffic Accident

RTA/C
Road Traffic Accident/Collision

RTP
Risk Treatment Plan

RTPC
Road Transport Policing Command

RTRA
Road Traffic Regulation Act

RUC
Royal Ulster Constabulary

RUI
Released Under Investigation

RVC
Repeat Victims Camera's

RVCTF
Racial & Violent Crime Task Force

RVP
Rendezvous Point

RWC
Rugby World Cup

S

S&S
Stop and Search

SA
Security Accreditation

SABs
Safeguarding Adult Boards

SABM
Set Asynchronous Balanced Mode Command

SAC
Scene Access Control

SAC
Special Address Comment

SAC
Safeguarding Adult Co-ordinator

SAC
Serious Acquisition Crime

SACMILL
Scientific Advisory Committee on the Medical Implication of Less – Lethal weapons

SAG
Safety Advisory Group

SAG
Specialist Advisory Group

SAL
Security Aspects Letter

SAMM
Support After Murder and Manslaughter

SAMURAI
Staff-support Associations Meeting Up Regularly and Interacting

SAN
Storage Area Network

SAO
Subject Access Office

SAR
Search and Rescue

SAR
Subject Access Request

SARCs
Sexual Assault Referral Centre

SAS
Staff Attitude Survey

SAT
System Acceptance Test

SB
Special Branch

SBG
Spit and Bite Guard

SBR
Strategic Business Requirements

SC
Security Check

SC
Special Constable

SC
Specialist Crime

SCAIDP
Specialist Child Abuse Investigation Development Programme

SCC

Surveillance Camera Commission

SCD
Specialist Crime Directorate

SCD
Sudden Death during Restraint

SCG
Serious Crime Group

SCH
Special Case Hearings

SCIE
Social Care Institute of Excellence

SCIT
Special Casework Investigation Team

SCO
Specialist Crime and Operations

SCRG
Specialist Crime Review Group

SCTI
Super Civil Anti-Trespass Injunction

SD
Sanction Detection

SDAR

Self Defence Arrest & Restraint

SDE
Self Defined Ethnicity

SDG
Service Delivery Group

SDHPPC
Safer Detention and Handling of Person in Police Custody

SDS
Short Data Service

SDVC
Specialist Domestic Violence Court

Secondary S/L
Secondary Service Level

SEC
Search Exemption Certificate

SEC
Standard Equitation Centre

SEG
Special Escort Group

SEG
Secure External Gateway

SEMIS

Security Evaluation of MPS Information Systems

SEN
Special Educational Needs

SeCOP
Service Reporting Code of Practice for Local Authorities

SERCO
Prisoner Escort Service

SERT
Special Entry & Recovery Team

SET
Special Enquiry Team

SFC
Strategic Firearms Commander

SFR
Streamlined Forensic Reporting

SGC
Shotgun Certificate

SGT
Sergeant

SHANKS
Seen, Heard, Actions, Conversation, Knowledge and Smell

SHPO
Sexual Harm Prevention Order

SHRA
Strategic Human Resources Adviser

SHRMT
Safety and Health Risk Management Team

SI
Special Investigations

SIA
Security Industry Accreditation Staff

SIAM
System Integration Application management

SIM
Senior Investigation Manager

SIM
Serenity Integrated Mentoring (Programme)

SIO
Senior Investigating Officer

SIP
Service Improvement Plan

SIRO
Senior Information Risk Owner

Sitrep
Situation Report

SIU
Service Intelligence Unit

SJT
Situational Judgement Test

S/L
Service Level

SLA
Service Level Agreement

SLO
Stores Liaison Officer

SLP
Strengthening Local Policing

SLSP
Systems Level Security Policy

SLT
Senior Leadership Team

SM
Security / System Manager

SMA
Social Media Applications

SMART
Specific, Measurable, Attainable, Relevant & Timely

SMB
School Management Board

SMB
Strategic Management Board

SME
Small and Medium Enterprises

SMF
Short Management Format

SMG
Santa Marta Group

SMIU
Serious Misconduct Investigation Unit

SMP
Select Medical Practitioners

SMP
Service Mobilisation Plan

SMP
Sustainability Management Plan

SMP
Sustainability Management Programme

SMS
Short Message Service

SMS
Safety Management System

SMT
Senior Management Team

SMTL
Social Media Team Leader

SNARL
South Norwood Animal Rescue League

SNBs
Safer Neighbourhood Boards

SNT
Safer Neighbourhood Team

SO
Specialist Operations

SOC
Serious and Organised Crime

SOCA
Serious Organised Crime and Police Act 2005

SOCA
Serious Organised Crime Agency

SOCO
Scenes of Crime Officer

SOCPV
Statement of Common Purpose & Values

SODFM
Scheme of Devolved Financial Management

SOECA
Sexual Offences Exploitation and Child Abuse

SOIE
Set Off In Error

SOIT
Sexual Offence Investigation Technique

SOLACE
Society of Local Authority Chief Executives

SOPO
Sexual Offences Prevention Order

SOPs
Standard Operating Procedures

SOR
Special Operations Room

SOR
Statement of Requirement

SOROC
Student Officer Record of Competence

SPDS
Service Policy Disclosure Statement

SPF
Security Policy Framework

SPG
Senior Pay Group

SPI
Statutory Performance Indicator

SPOC
Single Point of Contact

SPOs
Stalking Protection Orders

SPP
Strategic Policing Priorities

SPR
Strategic Policing Requirement

SPS
Senior Personal Secretary

SRB
Schedule Review Board

SRB
Single Regeneration Budget

SRC
Survivor Reception Centre

SRL
Strategic Resource Leverage

SRO
Station Reception Officer

SRO
Senior Responsibility Officer

SRR
Specialist Reconnaissance Regiment

SRS
Survivor Reception Centre Toolkit

SS
Special Schemes

SSA
Special Service Agreement

SSAB
Systems Security Assurance Board

SSCL
Shared Services Connected Ltd

SSG
Special Service Group

SSN
Special Scheme Number

SSO
Safer Schools Officers

SSOR
System Statement Of Requirements

SSP
Safer Schools Partnership

SSPS
Safer Sutton Partnership Service

SSS
Shared Support Services

STA
Single Tender Action

STAC
Scientific and Technical Advice Cell

STAC
Stalking Threat Assessment Centre

STADV
Standing Together Against Domestic Violence

STaN
Safer Travel at Night

STfA
Safer Travel for All

STL
Statutory Time Limit

STM
Strategic Training Meeting

STOPS
Search System Holding Records of Those Stopped and Searched

STRA
Strategic Threat and Risk Assessment

STRIDE
Strategic Inclusion Diversity and Equality Strategy

STT
Safer Transport Teams

STU
Specially Trained Unit

STX
Start of Frame Character

SUA

Small Unmanned Aircraft

SUDI
Sudden Unexpected Death in Infancy

Supt
Superintendent

SWA
Service Wide Assessment

SWG
Security Working Group

SWOT
Strengths, Weaknesses, Opportunities and Threats

SyAc
Security Assurance Co-ordinator

SyOPS
Security Operating Procedures

T

T&Cs
Terms and Conditions

TA
Tactical Advisor

TAAS
The Appropriate Adult Service

TACT
Terrorism Act 2000

TB
Training Board

TC
Terminal Closet

TC
Traffic Clerk

TCRAC
Temporary CRIMINT Remote Access

TCSU

Traffic Control Systems Unit

TCT
Town Centre Team

TDC
Training Detective Constable

TDIU
Telephone and Digital Investigation Unit

TDU
Training Design Unit

TER
Technology Equipment Room

TETRA
Terrestrial Trunked Radio

TFC
Tactical Firearms Commander

TF-CBT
Trauma Focused – Cognitive Behavioural Therapy

TFMV
Theft From a Motor Vehicle

THC
Tetrahydrocannabinol

THR
Transforming Human Resources

TIB
Telephone Investigation Bureau

TIC
Taken Into Consideration

TICs
Toxic Industrial Chemicals

TIMs
Toxic Industrial Materials

TIU
Telephone Investigation Unit

TMAG
Training Matters Action Group

TMB
Training Management Board

TNA
Training Needs Analysis

TNO
Total Notifiable Offence

TOC

Telephone Operator Centre

TOCU
Transport Operational Command Unit

TOM
Target Operating Model

TORS
Traffic Offence Reports

TP
Territorial Policing

TPAC
Tactical Pursuit and Containment

TP CBS OCU
Territorial Policing - Capability and Business Support Operational Command Unit

TPCCC
Territorial Police Command & Control Centre

TPCJ
Territorial Policing Criminal Justice

TPC&S
Territorial Policing Capability and Support

TPCSO
Traffic Police Community Support Officer

TPHQ
Territorial Police Head Quarters

TPP
Total Professionalism Programme

TPS
Telephone Preference Service (The)

TPU
Training Policy Unit

TRB
Technical Review Board

TRB
Total Resource Budget

TRR
Test Readiness Review

TS
Team Support

TSC
Traffic Support Clerk

TSD
Transport Services Department

TSG
Territorial Support Group

TSR
Tactical Safety Response

TSS
Trading Standards Service

TSSA
Trans Staff Support Association

TSU
Training Standards Unit

TTA
Time To Answer

TTCG
Tactical Tasking and Coordinating Group

TTL
Threats To Life

TTM
Tactical Tasking Meeting

TTP
Total Technology Programme

TTR
Terrestrial Trunk Radio

TU
Trails Unit

TUC
Trade Unions Congress

TUPE
Transfer of Undertakings (Protections of Employment)
Regulations

TV
Television

TVC
Total Victim Care

TVNP
Tele Vision Network Protocol

TW
Traffic Warden

TWM
Traffic Warden Manager

U

UAT
Unmanned Air Technology

UCO
Undercover Officer

UCR
Uniform Crime Reporting

UML
Unified Modelling Language

Unisys
Current C & C Supplier

UK
United Kingdom

UKBA
United Kingdom Border Agency

UKFPU
UK Football Policing Unit

UKHTC

United Kingdom Human Trafficking Centre

ULEZ
Ultra Low Emissions Zone

UME
Unlicensed Music Event

UoF
Use of Force

UoFPO
Use of Force for Public Order

UPS
Uninterrupted Power Supply

U/R
Unregistered

URN
Unique Reference Number

USS
User Satisfaction Survey

UTC
Universal Time Co-ordinate

V

VAF
Vulnerability Assessment Framework

VAP
Violence Against a Person

VAS
Voluntary Aid Societies

VAT
Value Added Tax

VAWG
Violence Against Women and Girls

VCD
Violent Crime & Directorate

VCOP
Victim Code of Practice

VCRM
Verification Cross Reference Matrix

VDD

Version Description Document

VDRS
Vehicle Defect Rectification Scheme

VDT
Visual Display Terminal

VDU
Visual Display Unit

VEL
Vehicle Excise Licence

VEM
Visible Ethnic Minorities

VfM
Value for Money

VFP
Visitors Firearms Permit

VIIDO
Visual Identification Image Detection Office

VIPER
Violent Persons Restraint

VIW
Victim, Informant, Witness

VPC

Volunteer Police Cadets

VPS
Victim Personnel Statement

VRES
Vehicle Recovery and Examination Service

VRM
Vehicle Registration Mark

VRR
Victims Right to Review

VS
Victim Support

VSP
Visitors Shotgun Permit

VSS
Victim Support Scheme

VTS
Vessel Traffic Services

VWI
Violence With Injury

W

WABCU
Western Area Basic Command Unit

WADS
Witness Album Display System

WAFTO
Working Away from the Office

WANS
Wide Area Networks

WBA
Work Based Assessors

WBA
Work Based Assignment

WBS
Work Breakdown Structure

WBSID
Work Breakdown Structure Identifier

WCU

Witness Care Unit

WDU
What's Driving Us

WECTU
West Extremism and Counter Terrorism Command Unit

WEEE
Waste Electrical & Electronic Equipment

WGA
Whole Government Accounts

WSU
Witness Support Unit

WTR
Working Time Regulations

Y

YACS
Youth And Community Section

YAP
Youth Advocate Programme

YBYL
Your Belt Your Life

YCP
Youth Crime Prevention

YCRS
Youth Crime Reduction Strategy

YET
Youth Engagement Team

YIP
Youth Inclusion Programme

YISP
Youth Inclusion & Support Panel

YJB
Youth Justice Board

YOIS
Young Offenders Information System

YOS
Youth Offending Service

YOTs
Youth Offending Teams

AFTERWORD

This is helping to pay my rent so
thank you for purchasing!

Strellus.com